W9-BCI-462

TOGETHER WE CAN!

ClassWide Peer Tutoring to Improve Basic Academic Skills

Charles R. Greenwood ▲ Joseph C. Delquadri ▲ Judith J. Carta

**SAINT MARY'S UNIVERSITY
OF MINNESOTA**

Copyright © 1997 by Charles R. Greenwood,
Joseph C. Delquadri, and Judith J. Carta

03 02 01 00 99   06 05 04 03 02

All rights reserved.

Contributions by Carmen Arreaga-Mayer, Granger Dinwiddie, Marleen Elliott,
R. Vance Hall, Verona Hughes, Debra Kamps, Frank Kohler,
Barbara Terry, and Dale Walker

This book contains student handout and transparency masters.
Permission is granted for the purchasing teacher to reproduce
the tools for use in his/her classroom only. No portion of this book
in whole or in part may be reprinted by any means without
the express written permission of the publisher.

Illustrations and cover art by Tom Oling
Cover design by Kimberly Harris
Typesetting and design by Cindy Young
Edited by Lynne Timmons

ISBN #1-57035-125-2

Printed in the United States of America

Published and Distributed by

Sopris West

4093 Specialty Place ▲ Longmont, CO 80504 ▲ (303) 651-2829
www.sopriswest.com

SAINT MARY'S UNIVERSITY
OF MINNESOTA

371. 394
G81

Apr-01
37897320

ACKNOWLEDGMENTS

The authors would like to thank the students, parents, and teachers of metropolitan Kansas City, Kansas, for their help, participation, and support of ClassWide Peer Tutoring (CWPT). Special thanks are owed Ms. Kathleen Stretton who, with Joseph Delquadri, helped design the first application of CWPT. Thanks are also owed Dr. R. Vance Hall who taught us that children do not become literate without massive "opportunities to respond" in home and school. Lastly, thanks are owed the National Institute of Children's Health and Human Development, and the Office of Special Education Programs, U.S. Department of Education for their support of programs that enabled the research and development that led to the CWPT program.

ABOUT THE AUTHORS

Charles Greenwood, Joseph Delquadri, and Judith Carta are researchers and colleagues at the Juniper Gardens Children's Project in Kansas City, Kansas, where they are also faculty members of the University of Kansas (Departments of Special Education and Human Development and Family Life). Each has a keen interest in the care and education of children in urban schools who are at-risk due to poverty, disability, and other risk factors associated with life in urban communities. Greenwood is an expert in elementary education and applied behavior analysis. Delquadri specializes in reading and the teaching of reading. Carta is an authority in early childhood education and in emergent literacy. Each conducts a program of research at the Juniper Gardens Children's Project, a load of teacher training, and supervision of graduate students.

INTRODUCTION

Together We Can! is a program that will help you simultaneously engage all the students in your class in a variety of academic tasks. These tasks can include fluent reading, rapid solutions to math facts and simple computations, and automatic spelling and reading of sight words.

With *Together We Can!* students interact directly with the learning task, rather than passively watching and listening to the teacher. Consequently, this program can double or triple the amount of practice that students typically receive in the basic subject areas.

THE PROCESS

The foundation of this program is ClassWide Peer Tutoring (CWPT), an instructional model based on reciprocal peer tutoring and group reinforcement. CWPT enables students to practice often and learn basic skills in a systematic, fun way. CWPT uses a combination of many effective instructional components. These components are:

1. Partner pairing;

2. Partners assigned to teams;

3. Two competing teams;

4. Immediate error correction;

5. Contingent point earning;

6. The posting of individual and team performance;

7. Distributed practice on weekly material to be learned;

8. High levels of mastery;

9. Systematic content coverage (e.g., spelling words, math facts, reading passages, and reading comprehension); and

10. Frequent testing.

WHAT MAKES CWPT UNIQUE?

CWPT differs from most other instructional methods in several important ways:

▶ CWPT uses peers to supervise responding and practice.

▶ CWPT uses a game-like format, including points and competing teams to motivate students and maintain their interest.

▶ CWPT uses a simple weekly evaluation plan to ensure gains in both individual and class progress.

WILL CWPT WORK?

Absolutely. The classwide peer tutoring model has been researched and used in classrooms since 1980. It has been repeatedly demonstrated that this process increases students' time on task and improves academic performance.Students in the CWPT groups increase the time they spend engaged in writing and academic talk, such as asking academic questions during spelling and mathematics lessons. Students also increase the time they spend on critical oral reading tasks.

Research proves that CWPT increases curriculum-based measures of achievement as well as standardized achievement test scores (see the Appendix). For example, students have increased their reading fluency (the rate of correctly read words per minute), increased the percentage of reading comprehension answers, increased the percentage of correctly spelled words and correct vocabulary words on weekly tests, and increased the percentage of correct math facts on weekly tests. Participating students have raised their grades through their higher weekly test performances. And, they remember skills they've learned later on (retention) and use them in other tasks (generalization). (For more informa-

tion about the research behind the CWPT procedure, see the Appendix.)

WILL ALL STUDENTS HAVE THE CHANCE TO BE SUCCESSFUL?

Yes, with CWPT the students' on-task behavior and time spent practicing academic tasks increases. This is true even for students who are the most difficult to motivate. For example, in one large-scale study (Greenwood, Delquadri, & Hall, 1989), disadvantaged students who were at risk for academic failure showed significant academic gains when this program was implemented in their classroom. These gains were shown in reading, mathematics, and language achievement as measured by the Metropolitan Achievement Test. Although these students were identified as being academically at risk, their achievement scores were in the normal range after four years of CWPT.

CWPT provides a systematic instructional environment for students in which they can master basic academic skills each day.

CWPT also reduces off-task, disruptive classroom behaviors. Students achieve more in less time when their teacher provides them with daily peer tutoring opportunities. And, because of its peer tutoring component, *Together We Can!* positively affects students' social interactions in the classroom. Working together in pairs to achieve a common team goal increases cooperation and other social skills.

WHAT ARE THE BENEFITS TO THE TEACHER?

CWPT is very flexible and adaptable. It is flexible in that it can be tailor-made to fit you, your classroom, and your students. It is easy to fit CWPT into your current teaching method, style, and program. Your students will help you tailor it to fit them—they will even come up with different ideas of how CWPT should run. They will propose effective reinforcers that they will work for, allowing you the flexibility to accommodate student diversity. CWPT can include almost everyone in a given classroom regardless of ability level.

CWPT is cost effective. With CWPT there are not a lot of extraneous parts, equipment, or materials to purchase. CWPT supplements whatever basal texts or materials you are currently using, and it adapts to any curricula. The only costs involved are the purchase of a regular kitchen timer if you don't already have one, and the reproduction of student handouts and transparency masters.

CWPT is easy to implement. Once you have taught your students to accurately perform the roles of both the tutor and tutee, the students can run the program on their own. It is very easy for a substitute teacher to run the program in your absence because the driving force is the one-on-one interactions by the students.

CWPT is time efficient. It can be implemented in 30-35 minute time blocks, and as students become more and more proficient in its operation, the time decreases. Within these short blocks, CWPT in-creases students' active exposure to the content, multiplying the opportunities that students have to respond. There are few teaching formats where students are so actively involved with the content directly, or where they are likely to experience such high rates of academic responding outside of the CWPT structure. These increased opportunities double and triple for most students, compared to what they would otherwise receive. CWPT is built on that old saying that "practice makes perfect."

USING THE PROGRAM

WHO CAN USE "TOGETHER WE CAN!"?

▶ Students in grades 1-8.

▶ Students with heterogeneous abilities within a single classroom; either regular or special education.

▶ Students with widely diverse skill levels, as in the case of today's mainstreamed, inclusionary classrooms.

▶ Low achievers and students who may be difficult to teach, such as students with learning disabilities and other mild disabilities and students with limited English proficiency.

HOW DOES "TOGETHER WE CAN!" WORK?

Basically, each student in the class is paired with a partner for a week. Each partner takes a turn tutoring the other by giving a word to be spelled, a math fact to solve, or by listening to a passage being read. The tutors award points to the tutees for correct answers and correctly read sentences, and tutees correct errors immediately. The teacher also awards points to tutors for appropriate behavior. All of the tutoring pairs comprise two teams in the classroom, and these two teams compete for points and social reinforcement.

Each week, students typically spend 30 to 35 minutes each day for four consecutive school days tutoring each other on a list of spelling words, math facts, or reading passages. The teacher tests students on the material on the fifth day, the students grade their partners' tests, points are awarded as appropriate, and the week's winning team is announced. Partners and team assignments change the following week.

CAN "TOGETHER WE CAN!" BE USED IN OTHER SUBJECT AREAS?

Certainly. This program can be applied to any subject areas in which facts are memorized or drilled, such as science, geography, history, foreign language, social studies, and so on.

WHAT MATERIALS ARE REQUIRED FOR "TOGETHER WE CAN!"?

Together We Can! is dependent on careful (but not difficult!) recordkeeping. Thirteen reproducible masters of charts and

student handouts designed specifically for the process are supplied in the back of this manual. You are encouraged to customize these in any way you wish by reproducing them, laminating those used repeatedly, enlarging any to poster size, making them into overhead transparencies, and so on. The only other supplies you will need are one kitchen timer, one calculator, and one stopwatch.

The 13 reproducibles included in this manual are:
For Teacher Use
   Monthly Subject List
   Percentage Conversion Table
   Happy Gram
   Bonus Point Reminder
   Reading Assignment Form
   Student Assessment Sheet
   Reading Rate Chart
For Student Use
   Weekly Tutoring List
   Tutoring Worksheet
   Tutoring Point Sheet
   Good Sports Handout
   Help Sign with Comprehension
   Questions

Also supplied are four 20" x 30" laminated posters for the teacher's use:

   Teams and Partners Chart
   Pretest/Posttest Score Chart
   Team Point Charts (2 provided—1
   for each team)

These charts and forms are indicated in bold type throughout this manual. Figure 1 illustrates how a CWPT Center might be designed as a focal point in the classroom.

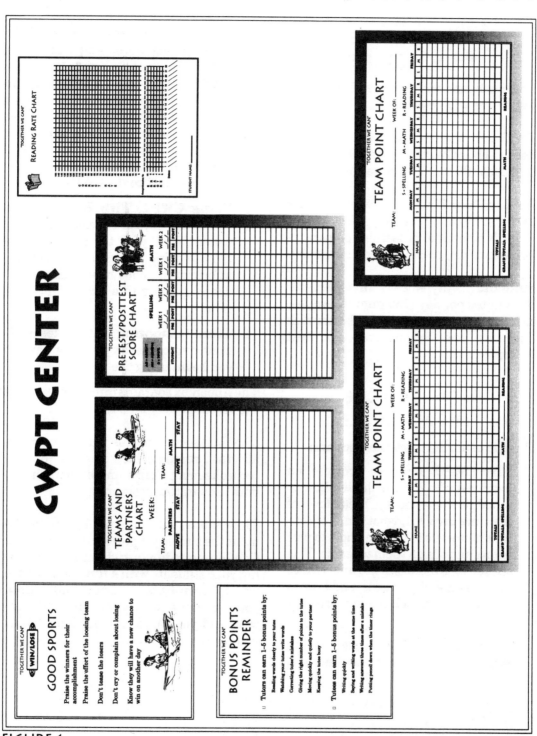

FIGURE 1

HOW MUCH TIME WILL THIS REQUIRE?

Not much, and your students' improving test scores will be worth it!

To Teach the Process to Your Students: Four CWPT lessons, 20 to 30 minutes each (80 to 120 minutes in all)

Weekly Prep Time: 45 to 60 minutes per CWPT subject (e.g., reading) being taught (identify content to be learned, prepare tutor's materials, prepare tutee's materials).

Students' Daily/Weekly Involvement: 30 minutes per day (150 minutes/week—includes tutoring sessions Monday through Thursday, and Friday pretest-posttest session).

HOW DO I USE THIS MANUAL?

There are four instructional sections:

1. **The CWPT Process** provides an overview of CWPT, including how to schedule the sessions, a breakdown of the time involved, what kinds of content materials to use, and how to pair tutors and assign them to teams. This section also discusses the importance of pretests and posttests, and how to give them for each subject area tutored.

2. **Teaching CWPT** leads you step by step through the process that will teach your students how to use CWPT with spelling words and math facts. Other topics include how to be a "good sport," how to move quietly and efficiently to their partners, what tutors and tutees do, how to win points, how to score, how to report their scores, and how to clean up. Included are instructions for demonstrating and having the students practice the CWPT process.

3. **Using CWPT With Reading** discusses the special considerations for using CWPT with the regular classroom reading program, and includes information about how to check students' reading rate and comprehension.

4. **Troubleshooting**, anticipates questions and concerns you may have as you begin using the program.

The Appendix contains information about the research that supports CWPT.

The final section of this manual contains all the reproducible masters of the recordkeeping charts and student handouts used in this program.

This manual will show you how to implement the simple yet powerful *Together We Can!* program in **your** classroom, providing your students with a fun and effective way to learn basic academic skills. Both you and your students will enjoy this process, and your students' academic gains will testify to its merit.

THE CWPT
PROCESS

THE CWPT PROCESS

HOW TO PAIR TUTORS

TUTORING PAIRS

In CWPT, students work with different partners of varying skill levels one week to next. In fact, it is never possible in one classroom to always have a higher-skilled tutor to match with each lower-skilled tutee. So CWPT relies on the materials, "loose" ability matching, and teacher monitoring to provide help and correct errors. The evidence shows that this combination works.

In CWPT, partners change each week to keep things interesting and to ensure that each student works with many other students over time. Thus, students learn to work cooperatively with their diverse peers on a daily basis. Teams change weekly, for similar reasons.

There are two approaches used to pair students for CWPT:

1. **Random pairing** means putting students together based on chance (e.g., drawing names from a hat). This method assures that, over time, all students will eventually work with every other student in the classroom. Using this method produces positive changes in how students view one another and improves their willingness to help and cooperate with one another.

2. **Skill pairing** means choosing students of nearly equal abilities to work with each other, or choosing a higher-skilled student to work with a lower-achieving student who needs more intensive help. This is called "cross-skill pairing."

In spelling and math, tutors are provided with the correct answers, so all students are in a position of checking the accuracy of their partner's written responses. Thus, in CWPT, students are paired randomly (with answers) in spelling and math.

In reading, tutors are not provided answers because it is a direct reading task. Students' reading ability must be considered when making pairing decisions, so students are normally paired by skill level (without answers). This procedure is used when reading abilities are very heterogeneous with very high and low students. Putting lower-achieving students together with higher level students improves the lower skilled students' opportunities for error correction and practice on troublesome words.

Sometimes you might choose to pair students randomly if they are reading the same materials (or in the same reading groups). You can stretch this rule a bit to allow pairing of students in adjacent levels of material or adjacent reading groups.

WEEKLY TEAMS

If you use random pairing, let students draw for pair assignments and then randomly assign the pairs to two teams. If you pair students by skill level, assign pairs randomly to the teams. This should create nearly equal teams. Give the teams fun names like the "Jazz" and the "Bulls," or let the winning team that week name the teams for the week ahead.

MOVE/STAY PAIRINGS

After the pairs and teams are determined, decide which half of the students will move and which half will stay in their places during CWPT. Post the **Teams and Partners Chart** (Figure 2) and indicate the "movers" and "stayers" on it.

Change pairs and teams each week to prevent boredom and to maintain high levels of interest.

"TOGETHER WE CAN"

TEAMS AND PARTNERS CHART

WEEK: _____11-12_____

TEAM: ____EAGLES____   TEAM: ____FALCONS____

PARTNERS		MATH	
MOVE	STAY	MOVE	STAY
Lori	Carmen	Lee	Ben
Brian	Ken	Dana	Pregash
Nathan	Joel	Robert	Michael
Jeremy	Ty	Peter	Abdoul
Kim	Kathy	Karen	Tina
Tran	Amy	Dalai	Deane
Anita	Barb	Ann	Sara/Erin

FIGURE 2

WHAT SUBJECTS TO TEACH

It is best to implement the program incrementally, one subject area at a time. It is recommended that you use CWPT first with spelling, then math facts, and finally, reading. The use of CWPT with reading is slightly different from the spelling and math applications, and is discussed further in Section 3.

Note: As a general rule, consider implementing a new subject area when: (1) you have observed gains in students' academic performances; and (2) you have observed that all students are playing the game correctly.

Divide your content material into lists of 10 to 30 items. Here are some considerations when developing your content lists:

1. Each item should require an overt response (e.g., orally spelling and writing words or reciting and writing math facts).

2. Items may be drawn from material already scheduled to be covered in a given week. For example, create your spelling list from vocabulary words used in the week's regular reading lesson.

3. Items should be drawn from those noted in grade level objectives, scope and sequence charts, students' IEPs, and texts available for your grade level.

4. The number of items on the list should be based generally on the observation that the lowest students can cover the list twice in ten minutes when they are the tutee.

5. The difficulty of the material on the list should be at 20 to 40% correct at **pretest** for the class average. Below 20% class average is too hard; above 40% is too easy.

Use the **Monthly Subject List** (Figure 3) to organize your content material, then transfer one week's list to the **Weekly Tutoring List** (Figure 4). You will be giving a copy of this weekly list to each pair of tutors. Tutors will use it to present each word or math fact and as a basis for making corrections.

"TOGETHER WE CAN"
MONTHLY SUBJECT LIST

TEACHER: Mr. Emery   MONTH: April   SUBJECT: Spelling

	WEEK 1: MONDAY DATE _/_/_	WEEK 2: MONDAY DATE _/_/_	WEEK 3: MONDAY DATE _/_/_	WEEK 4: MONDAY DATE _/_/_
1.	garden	wide	box	socks
2.	fox	side	sit	dance
3.	pretty	hide	fix	vine
4.	look	find	seek	rat
5.	farm	play	grade	dog
6.	mouse	hard	put	pig
7.	neat	can	place	line
8.	needs	fast	circle	mark
9.	fast	mother	girl	wagon
10.	woman	father	boy	shoes
11.	big			
12.	own			
13.	yes			
14.				

FIGURE 3

"TOGETHER WE CAN"
WEEKLY TUTORING LIST

TEACHER: Mr. Emery   MONTH: April   SUBJECT: Spelling

1.	garden	11.	big
2.	fox	12.	own
3.	pretty	13.	yes
4.	look	14.	
5.	farm	15.	
6.	mouse	16.	
7.	neat	17.	
8.	needs	18.	
9.	fast	19.	
10.	woman	20.	

FIGURE 4

WHEN TO TEACH

The time breakdown for each five-day tutoring session is shown in Figure 5. (However, the time requirement for reading is different and is covered in Section 3.)

Schedule time on the fifth day to test students on the materials previously tutored and to pretest the students on the new materials for the forthcoming week.

Keep in mind the following considerations when planning your schedule:

1. Each session should last approximately 30 to 35 minutes.

2. The spelling and math tutoring sessions most logically fit into times you've already designated for those subjects.

3. You will need to refer to your weekly lesson plan and your district's suggestions about time usage for each academic subject.

Once you have determined when you will fit the tutoring sessions into your weekly schedule, enter this information into your weekly schedule book.

PRETESTS AND POSTTESTS

PRETESTS

Pretests are evaluations of students' knowledge made before tutoring begins. Pretests cover content materials that will be tutored in the week ahead.

While posttest scores reveal how well students know a given set of words or math facts after CWPT, without pretest scores they do not give any indication of how much material students mastered in a week (their gains). Without pretests, you have no knowledge of how well the students knew the material before tutoring began or the effect of CWPT on students' learning. Pretests, therefore, provide a baseline against which you can

TIME REQUIRED (IN MINUTES)					
	DAY 1	DAY 2	DAY 3	DAY 4	DAY 5
Introduce new content	5				
Tutoring (1st student in pair)	10	10	10	10	
Tutoring (2nd student in pair)	10	10	10	10	
Point reporting and clean up	10	10	10	10	
Test over week's tutored material					15
Pretest over next week's materials					15
Totals	35	30	30	30	30

FIGURE 5

compare the scores after CWPT and know if the program is really working. In addition, the pretests indicate whether the content to be covered in tutoring will provide a challenge to the students. Don't get caught teaching material that most students already know! CWPT is designed to enable nearly all of the students to score 90% to 100% on their posttests after a week of tutoring. If you find that 70% of the class is scoring 90% or better on the pretest, the material on the week's list is too easy and needs to be changed in order for the students to benefit more from the tutoring activity. This can be done by adding words/items that the highest scoring students do not know. By adding unknown words/items to the tutoring lists, the difficulty factor is increased for the entire class. A class average of 20% to 40% on the pretest is

appropriate. Tutoring should be used to teach new material and not just as a means for reviewing what the students already know.

Give a pretest on new material on the fifth day of a tutoring week. The tests can be graded by the teacher or could be graded by the students and reviewed for accuracy by the teacher. Record the pretest percentage scores on the **Pretest/ Posttest Score Chart** (Figure 6).

The pretest results should be reviewed frequently by the teacher. If it is apparent that most students in the class know the words/items, add more advanced items to the list for tutoring each week.

"TOGETHER WE CAN"
PRETEST/POSTTEST SCORE CHART

AB = ABSENT
MS = MISSING
☆ = 100%

STUDENT	SPELLING WEEK 1 PRE	SPELLING WEEK 1 POST	SPELLING WEEK 2 PRE	SPELLING WEEK 2 POST	MATH WEEK 1 PRE	MATH WEEK 1 POST	MATH WEEK 2 PRE	MATH WEEK 2 POST
Amy	20	85	30	☆	25	☆	10	☆
Anita	30	☆	35	☆	25	☆	0	75
Arturo	10	90	20	☆	20	85	5	80
Barb	10	90	20	90	30	☆	10	80
Carmen	AB	AB	AB	☆	20	90	0	90
Elaine	15	90	15	80	30	☆	10	☆
Hee	0	70	MS	85	10	☆	15	☆
Jennifer	10	80	15	☆	40	90	20	☆
Morgan	15	95	40	☆	15	80	5	☆

(SPELLING columns: WEEK 1 __/__/__ , WEEK 2 __/__/__ ; MATH columns: WEEK 1 __/__/__ , WEEK 2 __/__/__)

FIGURE 6

POSTTESTS

Posttests are tests given on the content (e.g., spelling words or math problems) taught during the tutoring sessions, Day 1 through Day 4. The items on these tests are the same as those on the tutoring lists, but presented in a different order.

Posttests provide feedback on whether students have mastered the content on the tutoring lists. If most of the students are not getting perfect scores on the posttests, you will need to closely examine the tutoring sessions during the week for possible problems.

The posttest should be given on the fifth day of the tutoring week in the same fashion as the pretest. It is recommended that the posttest be given first, then the pretest. The tests can be graded by the teacher or could be graded by the students and reviewed for accuracy by the teacher. The posttest percentage scores should be recorded on the **Pretest/Posttest Score Chart**. Pretests and posttests can be given on the same sheet of paper, the pretest on the front and the posttest on the back.

The posttest results should be reviewed frequently by the teacher. If 70% of the class is not scoring 90% or higher on the posttest, you should consider assessing the quality of the peer tutoring they are receiving; if it's acceptable, consider decreasing the math problem or word difficulty.

RECORDING TEST SCORES

1. When you post students' pretest and posttest scores, you will need to convert them from raw scores to percentages. Use the **Percentage Conversion Table** for this purpose.

2. Record all percentage scores on the **Pretest/Posttest Score Chart**. This chart is posted publicly in the classroom (see Appendix).

3. Record a ☆ for anyone who earned 100%.

4. Determine which students gained at least 20 percentage points from pretest to posttest.

5. Determine from the **Pretest/Posttest** Score Chart who has earned a **Happy Gram** (Figure 7) for the week by using the following criteria:

   - Anyone earning 100% on the posttest.

   - Anyone improving their score from the pretest to the posttest by 20% or more.

FIGURE 7

TEACHING CWPT

TEACHING CWPT

This section contains the classroom exercises needed to teach your students to perform the tutor and tutee roles and to provide the opportunity for practicing CWPT. It uses spelling and math to illustrate. Teaching CWPT for reading generally follows the same sequence, the same procedures, and uses the same tutoring point sheet, but there are some special considerations which are covered in Section 3. These exercises are to be completed before you actually attempt to implement the tutoring. Your students must be able to perform these exercises well in order for CWPT to be a success the first time it is implemented. These exercises are divided into four general lessons entitled: (1) Learning About CWPT; (2) Moving to a Partner; (3) Play and Practice; and (4) Reporting Points and Cleaning Up.

It is recommended that you introduce and practice these procedures (one at a time, one per day) before going through the entire CWPT process. This can be done in the week prior to implementing CWPT sessions for the first time. These activities help the class ease into CWPT with

knowledge of its essential parts. Depending on the age and sophistication of your students, adjust the level of these activities as necessary.

SESSION 1:
LEARNING ABOUT CWPT

The initial step is to give students a clear explanation of what the peer tutoring game is. This includes teaching about winning and losing, and what it means to be a "good sport." For first graders, CWPT may be the first team game they learn.

MATERIALS NEEDED

None

THE TUTORING GAME

Introduce *Together We Can!* to the students by explaining that *Together We Can!* is a game that makes learning fun and interesting. Let them know that they will work together and help each other study spelling, math, and (eventually) reading. This is called "peer tutoring." Describe to the students these elements of peer tutoring:

1. The tutor acts as the teacher.

2. The tutee is the student and takes direction from the tutor.

3. Tutor/tutee pairs are chosen each week.

4. Both members of a pair are always on the same team.

5. Two teams are appointed each week.

6. Pairs and teams change each week.

TEAMS WIN AND LOSE

Next, explain that the teams compete to win by correctly spelling words or solving math problems. The team that earns the most points wins. Ensure that students understand these points:

1. Each student should expect to be on winning and losing teams. It is not possible for everyone to be on a winning team all the time. (Students should expect to win about half the time.)

2. The reward for the winning team will be applause for their fine achievement.

3. The losing team is also applauded for their fine effort to win.

4. Students are always expected to be good sports about winning or losing the tutoring game.

Distribute the **Good Sports** student handout (Figure 8) and discuss what each

"TOGETHER WE CAN"

◄▣ WIN/LOSE ▣►

GOOD SPORTS

Praise the winners for their accomplishment

Praise the effort of the losing team

Don't tease the losers

Don't cry or complain about losing

Know they will have a new chance to win on another day

FIGURE 8

bulleted statement means. Have several students explain what good sports do when they win and when they lose. Praise students who give answers that fit the premise about good sports just discussed. Have the students practice being good sports in the following scenario (write on the chalkboard to make the example clearer).

The right side of the room is the "Asteroids" team and the left side is the "Meteors" team. They have just completed playing *Together We Can!* The Asteroids scored 200 points, and the Meteors scored 178 points.

Lead the class through the following observations and responses:

1. The Asteroids won because they earned the most points.

   Have the class applaud the winning Asteroids team.

2. The Meteors came very close to winning—only a 22-point difference.

Have the class applaud the effort of the Meteors.

Practice this scenario several times with several different outcomes (i.e., one team wins by one point, there is a tie, both teams win once and lose once, and so on). By practicing, you will prepare the students for the correct response at the end of each game. This training is very important for students who have not participated on teams before. Remember to acknowledge both winning and losing teams at the end of each game, and praise students who are good sports. Obviously, this is important for the continuing satisfaction of the students with the game.

SESSION 2:
MOVING TO A PARTNER

One of the first things students must do in order to tutor is to move and sit next to their partner—the person they will be working with.

MATERIALS NEEDED

Teams and Partners Chart

MOVING AND STAYING

Using the **Teams and Partners Chart**, have the students note who their partners are. Explain the rules of moving:

1. No one is to move until the teacher gives the signal. The signal is when the teacher says, "Ready, move."

2. The "movers" are not to take chairs with them; rather, they are to find a chair near their partners.

3. Students who stay are to look for an empty chair near them for their partners.

4. Moving should be quiet and completed quickly without running or disruption.

Now have the students practice moving:

1. Obtain the students' attention— have all the students look at you and listen.

2. Briefly review the Move/Stay procedures. Make sure each "mover" knows where he or she is going ("Latisha—who is your partner?").

3. Tell the "movers" to stand.

4. Give the students the signal to move to their tutoring partners. Say "Ready, move." Require the "movers" to stand next to their partners while you check to see that all students have partners and seats. Praise the "movers" for quick and quiet moving, and praise their partners for remaining quiet while waiting for the "movers" to arrive.

5. Tell the students to sit next to their partners.

Praise students who move correctly. If they move incorrectly, have the students return to their original seats and practice moving again.

Have the students practice moving several times until you are satisfied they can move properly. Change the partners on the chart and try it again! Then go on to the next task that you have planned for the day.

SESSION 3:
PLAY AND PRACTICE

This is the part you and your students have been eagerly anticipating—learning to play the game!

MATERIALS NEEDED

- ▶ **Weekly Tutoring List** (use Spelling for the first game; 1 per pair),
- ▶ **Tutoring Worksheet** (1 per student),
- ▶ **Tutoring Point Sheet** (1 per student),
- ▶ **Help Sign** (1 per pair),
- ▶ **Timer** (1)

Note: You may wish to laminate the **Tutoring Point Sheets** in order to reuse them. The students will need erasable pens, markers, or crayons for marking the points, and paper towels to clean off the laminated sheets at the end of the game.

PART 1:
A MATTER OF FORM

Before teaching your students how to play the tutoring game, become familiar with the **Tutoring Worksheet** (Figure 9) and the **Tutoring Point Sheet** (Figure 10). When making copies for your students' use, you may want to use different colored paper for each sheet. Also, make a transparency of each of these forms to use with an overhead projector when you are explaining the game to your class.

"TOGETHER WE CAN"

TUTORING WORKSHEET

STUDENT: Danny DATE: 11/9 SUBJECT: Spelling

		CORRECTION PRACTICE 1	2	3
1.	garden			
2.	fox			
3.	pretty			
4.	lok	look	look	look
5.				
6.				
7.				
8.				
9.				
10.				
11.				
12.				
13.				

FIGURE 9

Tutoring Worksheet

When the tutor reads the spelling word, the tutee spells the word aloud and writes it on the numbered line in the left-hand column. If the spelling is correct, the next word is written on line 2, and so on. Whenever a word is misspelled, the tutor says the word again and spells it. The tutee then spells the word aloud while writing it three times under the columns entitled "Correction Practice."

Tutoring Point Sheet

Tutors record the number of points earned by the tutee by marking through the appropriate number of points on the point sheet. The point sheet is cumulative so that at the end of the session the last number marked is the total points earned. Thus, the addition of points is not required for each student to arrive at a point total. For example, each time a tutee spells a word correctly, the tutor marks through two points on the point sheet. Figure 11 illustrates a point sheet after the tutee correctly spelled three words in a row.

When the tutee makes an error and successfully completes the correction procedure (i.e., spelling the word correctly three times), the tutor circles one point. Figure 12 illustrates the point sheet after the tutee made a mistake, but successfully completed the correction. However, if the student makes an error during the correction procedure, he or she will not earn any points for that word.

Times Through the Material

Tutors also record each time the Tutee completes the list by marking each time through. This indicates the degree of practice obtained by each student in ten minutes.

"TOGETHER WE CAN"

TUTORING POINT SHEET

STUDENT: ______ DATE: ______ SUBJECT: ______

TIMES THROUGH: 1 2 3 4 5 6 7 8 9 10

1	2	3	4	5	6	7	8	9	10	11	12
13	14	15	16	17	18	19	20	21	22	23	24
25	26	27	28	29	30	31	32	33	34	35	36
37	38	39	40	41	42	43	44	45	46	47	48

FIGURE 10

"TOGETHER WE CAN"

TUTORING POINT SHEET

STUDENT: Danny DATE: 11/9 SUBJECT: Spelling

TIMES THROUGH: 1 2 3 4 5 6 7 8 9 10

~~1~~	~~2~~	~~3~~	~~4~~	~~5~~	~~6~~	7	8	9	10	11	12
13	14	15	16	17	18	19	20	21	22	23	24
25	26	27	28	29	30	31	32	33	34	35	36
37	38	39	40	41	42	43	44	45	46	47	48

FIGURE 11

"TOGETHER WE CAN"

TUTORING POINT SHEET

STUDENT: Danny DATE: 11/9 SUBJECT: Spelling

TIMES THROUGH: 1 2 3 4 5 6 7 8 9 10

~~1~~	~~2~~	~~3~~	~~4~~	~~5~~	~~6~~	(7)	8	9	10	11	12
13	14	15	16	17	18	19	20	21	22	23	24
25	26	27	28	29	30	31	32	33	34	35	36
37	38	39	40	41	42	43	44	45	46	47	48

FIGURE 12

PART 2:
HOW TO PLAY
"TOGETHER WE CAN!"

When you have all the students' attention, begin instructing them in how to play the *Together We Can!* game. Pass out the **Weekly Tutoring List**, **Tutoring Worksheets**, **Tutoring Point Sheets**, marking pens, paper towels, and **Help Signs**.

Let's Play *Together We Can!*

▼ Teacher ▼

"The object of the game is to earn as many points for yourself and for your team as you can. You earn two points for every word you spell correctly. If you misspell a word, you can practice spelling the word correctly three times and then earn one point.

Every day you work with your tutoring partner. Every day you will have the opportunity to be both the tutor and the tutee. The tutor is the person who reads the spelling words from the **Weekly Tutoring List**. *The tutee writes the word on the* **Tutoring Worksheet** *and at the same time spells the word out loud. The tutor checks what the tutee has written against the word on the* **Weekly Tutoring List**. *If it is right, the tutor says, 'Correct, two points.' The tutor then marks through two numbers on the* **Tutoring Point Sheet**. *The tutor then presents the next word on the list."*

Demonstrate how words are written on a **Tutoring Worksheet** and how points are marked on a **Tutoring Point Sheet** using transparencies you have prepared for an overhead projector. Make sure all students understand the process.

▼ Teacher ▼

"If the word is spelled incorrectly, the tutor says the word again and spells it slowly for the tutee. The tutee can then get one point by spelling the word out loud and writing the word correctly three times on the **Tutoring Worksheet**. *If the practices are all correct, the tutor circles one point on the* **Tutoring Point Sheet**. *If, however, one of the three practices is misspelled, the tutee does not earn any points. The tutor pronounces and spells the missed word correctly and then goes to a new word on the tutoring list."*

Demonstrate how corrections are made on the transparency. Then ask a student to join you at the front of the class. Using a **Weekly Tutoring List**, **Tutoring Worksheet**, and **Tutoring Point Sheet** prepared for an overhead projector, demonstrate how to play the game.

Sample Teacher/Student Demonstration

Tutor: (reading from tutoring list) "Spell 'time'."

Tutee: "t-i-m-e"

Tutor: "Correct, two points. Spell 'once'."

Tutee: "w-o-n-s"

Tutor: "No, it's o-n-c-e."

Tutee: "o-n-c-e, o-n-c-e, o-n-c-e"

Tutor: "Correct, one point. Spell 'list'."

Tutee: "l-i-s-t-e"

Tutor: "Stop, the correct word is l-i-s-t."

Tutee: "l-i-s-t, l-i-s-t, l-o-s-t"

Tutor: "No, you spelled the last one wrong. It's l-i-s-t. Zero points."

The tutor presents a new word and continues the process.

▼ Teacher ▼

*"After ten minutes, the tutor and tutee trade jobs. If the tutor goes through all the words before the ten minutes are up, he or she starts again at the top of the list. I will set a timer (show the timer) and when it rings, the tutees immediately stop writing and the tutors write the last marked number on the back of the tutee's point sheet (demonstrate with the **Tutoring Point Sheet** on the overhead projector). Then I will re-set the timer for another ten minutes. This time, those who wrote the words first will now read the words, and those who were reading the words now get to write the words."*

Ask for questions and ensure all students are clear on how to play the game. Highlight the following points for them.

▼ Teacher ▼

"Tutors, when giving words to your tutee, be sure to say them clearly. Listen carefully to your tutee's response. Tell your tutee quickly if the word was spelled correctly of if he or she will need to try again for one point.

Tutees, it will help you to make points if you work quickly and do what your tutor says. To earn points, be sure to spell a word out loud as you write it. If you don't know how to spell a word, try to spell it anyway. If you spell it incorrectly, your tutor will spell it for you and you can still try for one point by spelling the word out loud and writing it three times correctly.

For both tutors and tutees, if the tutor cannot read the word or either of you has a question, raise the **Help Sign** *(see Figure 13) so the teacher can help you.*

Tutors and tutees can earn bonus points from the teacher for playing the game right."

FIGURE 13

PART 3: TWO-STUDENT DEMONSTRATION

After you and a student have completed the demonstration to your satisfaction, have two students volunteer to demonstrate the game. Have one student act as the tutor and the other act as the tutee. As they play the game, give instructions and feedback. Praise them for playing correctly. Have the students trade roles and play the game again. Then ask another pair to demonstrate. Encourage your most low-achieving students to demonstrate how the game is played so you are sure everyone understands.

PART 4: ENTIRE CLASS PRACTICE

Ask the students to move to their partners (as they did previously) to practice tutoring for the first time. Move among them, answer questions, and give feedback. Award bonus points to both tutors and tutees you observe engaged in the correct tutoring behavior.

Bonus Points

Post the **Bonus Points Reminder Chart** (Figure 14) where your students can see it easily.

"TOGETHER WE CAN"

BONUS POINTS REMINDER CHART

Tutors can earn 1-5 bonus points by:

Reading words clearly to your tutee

Watching your tutee write words

Correcting tutee's mistakes

Giving the right number of points to the tutee

Moving quickly and quietly to your partner

Keeping the tutee busy

Tutees can earn 1-5 bonus points by:

Writing quickly

Saying and writing words at the same time

Writing answers three times after a mistake

Putting pencil down when the timer rings

FIGURE 14

Teachers will want to award one to five bonus points TO TUTORS for:

► clear, accurate reading of spelling words

"Dana, you're really reading those spelling words clearly. Two points for you!"

► watching tutees' written responses

"Mai, I'm going to give you three points for watching Luz write those words."

► correcting mistakes

"Samantha, great job correcting Vu's mistake. Four bonus points!"

▶ giving the right number of points

"Darnel, you're giving Stephanie the right number of points every time. Three points for you!"

▶ starting list over

"Bridger, you remembered to start the list again. Three bonus points!"

▶ moving quickly and quietly to partner

"One point for Thomas, Allie, Shanay, Jesse, Meg, and Gustavo for moving to their partners so quickly and quietly."

▶ keeping the tutee busy

"Marie, three points for keeping Tyrone busy and on task."

Teachers will want to award one to five bonus points TO TUTEES for:

▶ writing quickly

"Sam is really writing his words fast. He gets four bonus points."

▶ spelling aloud and writing words at the same time

"Markus, you're remembering to spell the word as you write it. That earns you two bonus points!"

▶ writing answers three times after a mistake

"Cheyenne, you are writing the correct answer three times—three points for you!"

▶ putting pencil down when the timer rings

"Jason, Ana, Isabel, Gao, Orlando, Jennifer—three bonus points for putting your pencils down immediately when the timer rang."

Mark the bonus points on the student's **Tutoring Point Sheet** by marking through the appropriate number of points after the last point marked by the tutor. Use a marking pen of a different color, so it is evident how many bonus points students earn.

If students are playing the game wrong, stop them and re-explain. Then ask them to play again and praise the correct form. Continue this until you are satisfied that all students understand.

SESSION 4:
REPORTING POINTS AND CLEANING UP

At the end of the tutoring session, the students will report their points out loud. Post the points by their names on the **Team Point Chart**.

MATERIALS NEEDED

▶ Completed **Tutoring Point Sheets**,

▶ **Team Point Chart** (1 for each team),

▶ Calculator

Your goal with point recording is to make it as brief as possible, no longer than five or ten minutes. A low noise level is essential to achieve this goal. Call on each student to report aloud his or her score. Students do not return to their original seats until point reporting has been completed and a winning team announced.

Note: If you use laminated **Tutoring Point Sheets**, the class can be quietly cleaning them off as the teacher calls each student for the point total. Have the students write the number of points on the back of their point sheets to prevent accidental erasing of the point totals. The cleanup should be done quietly.

DAYS ONE THROUGH FOUR

On the first through the fourth days, students will report to you their points earned during tutoring. You record these totals on the **Team Point Chart**, first for one team and then for the other (Figure 15). Be sure to make adjustments for triads (see Troubleshooting section). When you have finished recording and adding the points, record the team totals and announce the winning team for that session. Lead the students in applause for both teams.

Point Reporting Procedure

Teacher moves to the **Team Point Chart** with calculator in hand.

Teacher: "All eyes on me! Good, you are all looking."

Tell the students they can clean up quietly by wiping off their laminated sheets. Pick one of the teams and call the names as listed down the team's chart. As each student reports, write in the number of points on the **Team Point Chart** and enter it into your calculator or have a student helper enter the points.

Teacher: "We now have five (or 10) minutes to clean up and report points." (Set the timer for five minutes.) "J.T."

J.T.: "Nineteen points." (Write 19 and enter it into the calculator.)

Teacher: "Good, that's better than you did yesterday."

Teacher: "Shea."

Shea: "Fifty-two." (Write 52 and enter it into the calculator.)

Teacher: "Great! That's the best you've had all week!"

Teacher: "Jason."

Jason: "Forty-seven." (Write 47 and enter it into the calculator.)

Teacher: "Very good!"

"TOGETHER WE CAN"

TEAM POINT CHART

TEAM: Asteroids WEEK OF: 11/2

S-PELLING M-MATH R-READING

	MONDAY			TUESDAY			WEDNESDAY			THURSDAY			FRIDAY		
NAME	S	M	R	S	M	R	S	M	R	S	M	R	S	M	R
Amy															
Angelo															
Brian															
Chen															
Dana															

FIGURE 15

DAY FIVE

On the fifth day, students report to you a point score based on their posttest performance. The points that are reported are double the number correct (i.e., If Dan got 14 of 15 spelling words correct on the posttest, he would receive 28 points). Doubling the points will give students a score somewhat comparable to points earned on prior days, thus emphasizing the value of good posttest scores. You record the posttest scores on the **Team Point Chart**, then calculate the week totals and grand totals and announce the winning team. Praise the winning team and remind everyone to applaud. Everyone then applauds everyone else for trying hard. (Posttest scores are also recorded on the **Pretest-Posttest Score Chart**).

If the students become disruptive during the reporting process, stop and simply state the number of minutes remaining on the timer for point reporting. Resume when the classroom is again quiet and the students are looking at you.

Practice awarding points with the students until you are satisfied with the amount of time it takes and with the noise level during the reporting. Then proceed with incorporating *Together We Can!* into your daily routine, using students' scores to help determine their grade for the reporting period.

Many teachers find it helpful to distribute packets of tutoring materials to their students at the beginning of the tutoring session. The materials can be packed into 9" x 12" envelopes (one envelope per tutoring pair) and should include:

▶ 1 **Weekly Tutoring List** (e.g., spelling words)

▶ 1 **Help Sign** with comprehension questions on the back

▶ 2 Markers

▶ 2 **Tutoring Worksheets** (consumables or laminated)

▶ 2 **Tutoring Point Sheets** (laminated)

▶ 2 Paper towels or cloth for clean-up

These are all the steps needed to teach your students to carry out spelling CWPT; you are now ready to begin full classroom implementation. It is recommended that you start on the first Monday following these lessons, because your students will be ready. Following two or three weeks of full spelling CWPT implementation, you should find that your students are increasingly familiar with the procedures and that their spelling scores following a week's tutoring are much improved and continuing to improve. You also may find it necessary to review the tutoring procedures for some students during this intitial time, particularly carrying out the error correction steps or the point reporting steps. Consider providing a review to the whole class each week, pointing out areas of excellence and areas needing improvement. For students having specific problems, tutor with them one-on-one, or let them tutor you one-on-one so they can receive practice, correction, and feedback from you in the context of carrying out the tutoring steps. This will firm up the skills needed to use CWPT successfully.

As your students develop success and enthusiasm for spelling CWPT, consider using CWPT with math. Using the same format for identifying spelling words relevant to your content goals (review the earlier chapter "The CWPT Process," including the **Monthly Subject List** and **Weekly Tutoring Lists**), identify the math problems to be used in math tutoring. You must conduct a pretest on this material prior to the first tutoring week to assure its appropriateness using the same rules used in spelling.

Beginning the math program is simply a matter of announcing it to the students and allocating space on the charts for both spelling and math point recording and test score recording.

PLAYING 'TOGETHER WE CAN!"

STEP 1. Move to tutoring positions.

    A. Get the attention of all students.

    B. Briefly review the Move/Stay procedure.

    C. Tell the "movers" to stand.

    D. Give the students the signal to move to their partners.

    E. Tell the students to sit next to their partners.

STEP 2. Get ready for tutoring.

    A. Pass out materials. (Put in packets to facilitate this step, 1 packet/pair)

        1. Weekly Tutoring List

        2. Tutoring Worksheets

        3. Tutoring Point Sheets

        4. Help Signs and comprehension questions

        5. Marking pens and paper towels

    B. Set the timer and give the signal to begin tutoring.

STEP 3. Play *Together We Can!*
Have students write their point totals on the back of the **Tutoring Point Sheets** when the timer sounds.

STEP 4. Clean up, report points, and declare the winning team.

STEP 5. Make transitions to the next class activity.

CLASSWIDE PEER TUTORING
GENERAL TIPS

▶ Be excited, and have fun.

▶ Praise and reward good tutoring behavior.

▶ Try to make the teams as equal in ability as possible.

▶ Alternate starting from the top and the bottom of the tutoring list each day.

▶ Give the posttest items in an entirely different order than the tutoring lists.

▶ To reduce cheating on the point totals, spot check students randomly every now and then.

▶ Reward top point earners by letting them name their team once in a while.

▶ If tutoring goes well, and all students are responding well, let them choose their own partner for the week.

▶ Award the winning team with lining up first to go to lunch, recess, or home on the days they win.

▶ Reinforce the losing team by expressing your confidence that they can out-score the winning team the next day.

▶ Stress the proper care of the tutoring materials. Always recap the pens so that they will not dry out, and clean off the laminated sheets carefully so that they will not tear.

▶ Work out a quick and simple way of passing out the tutoring packets.

▶ Place the students' names on the worksheets and point sheets with masking tape and they will never have to write or erase their name from the sheet.

▶ Use a different colored marker than the students to mark bonus points.

USING CWPT
WITH READING

USING CWPT
WITH READING

USING CWPT WITH READING

Although CWPT with reading can be implemented independently, it is highly recommended that you first complete several successful weeks of spelling and/or math CWPT. Although the reading tutoring process is very similar to spelling and math CWPT, it is different enough to warrant its own section. (In this section, only those procedures that differ from those discussed earlier will be covered.):

IMPLEMENTING READING CWPT

MATERIALS NEEDED

▶ Classroom reading materials,

▶ **Reading Assignment Forms**,

▶ **Tutoring Point Sheets**,

▶ **Team Point Chart**,

▶ Calculator,

▶ Minute Timer

SCHEDULE TIME FOR READING CWPT

CWPT with reading has been designed to be used with your existing reading program. The heart of the program involves providing all students daily oral reading and comprehension engagement on units of the text, or other materials, you are currently using. As such, practice is based on the instructional goals of the reading program you are implementing. In operation, reading CWPT becomes dependent on your basal reading program. Thus, it needs to be used in association with your regular reading period, utilizing materials and focusing on skills included in your lesson plans.

Planning the number of school days for tutoring is easier when Reading Peer Tutoring (RPT) coincides with the number of days that are typically devoted to covering a unit or chapter in a basal reader. Here, a day is defined as a school day in which a full reading period of the standard amount of time (e.g., 60 minutes) is held. As it turns out, almost all teachers allot, on average, five days per unit, or one week per unit. In order to gain an optimal effect from RPT, spend five days per unit, the number of days that tutoring needs to be held in order to be effective. Completing one unit per week affords four days of tutoring on passages connected with the unit, and four days of tutoring is the magic number in terms of student results. It becomes extremely critical for students in your class who have lower reading skill levels. The fifth day is designated as the students' assessment day.

Given the above consideration, a time breakdown is provided in Figure 16. This example illustrates a 60-minute period in which a CWPT in reading lasts for 35 to 40 minutes. Skill instruction involves meeting with students, whole-class, or in small skill level groups. Independent seatwork involves work in workbooks, skill sheets, and other activities. It assumes that five days will be used to cover a unit.

"TOGETHER WE CAN" WEEKLY TIME REQUIRED (IN MINUTES)					
ACTIVITY	**DAY 1**	**DAY 2**	**DAY 3**	**DAY 4**	**DAY 5**
Skills Instruction and new content, independent seatwork	20	20	20	20	20
Oral Reading Tutoring (first student in pair)	10	10	10	10	
Comprehension Tutoring (first student in pair)	5	5	5	5	
Oral Reading Tutoring (second student in pair)	10	10	10	10	
Comprehension Tutoring (second student in pair)	5	5	5	5	
Team Points	10	10	10	10	
Student Assessment					40
NOTE: In this example, new vocabulary words and other skills to be integrated need to be introduced before the first CWPT session corresponding to the planned unit, lesson, or chapter.					

FIGURE 16

In the preceding example, teachers generally provide necessary instruction for the next week's unit on Friday, or Day 5. This is characterized by introducing vocabulary words, specific phonics skills, comprehension instruction, and skills that are introduced and reinforced in the unit. On tutoring days, the first 20 minutes can also be used to introduce or review these skills. Often during this time, teachers provide a mini-lesson to the entire class based upon a unit skill and let the students know that during tutoring they will be expected to use the skill, which will result in bonus points from the teacher. This can be especially useful during the comprehension component when the teacher expects a specific type of question, or expects the students to attend to specific content. For example, "I will be giving bonus points to students who ask questions related to the Emancipation Proclamation" cues the students to what to read for during the tutoring activity.

The student assessment block is for listening to students read passages they have previously practiced during CWPT.

Teachers normally take about five minutes per student so the time block in Figure 16 would allow for up to eight students. When more students are to be assessed, it can be completed on other tutoring days, at another time of the day, or on alternating weeks. This block must occur at least once a week in order to obtain a posttest check on reading progress. During this time, you will conduct a reading rate check on a one-minute reading by each target student. This check serves as an evaluation of the effect that tutoring has had on the student's speed, fluency, and accuracy. You will also conduct an evaluation of the student's reading comprehension during this time. More on selecting and evaluating target students for reading rate checks will be covered later.

There are two options for incorporating CWPT with reading:

1. As a supplement to the existing reading program.

    As a supplement, CWPT can be scheduled to replace some nonreading instruction (e.g., handwriting). This option increases the total time allocated to reading instruction. The goal of CWPT is to remediate student fluency by increasing both the time available and opportunities for direct reading practice.

    If small group reading is used, CWPT should occur before scheduling of the small groups, so that students are fluent with the material they will read aloud during the groups. This method aids successful performance during reading groups. Some teachers have scheduled skill introduction lessons once or twice a week, sandwiched between CWPT sessions covering appropriate story passages containing these skills.

    In a reading program centered on programmed reading materials, CWPT may be used to increase direct practice of the reading text. In this format, reading in programmed workbooks may be followed by CWPT, which is followed by seatwork.

2. As a replacement for one or more elements of an existing program.

As a replacement program, CWPT is scheduled instead of some or all existing elements of the conventional reading program for weekly times (Figure 16). In the traditional three-reading-group basal reading program, teachers often replace their reading group time with CWPT. They retain the skill introduction element (e.g., an entire group lecture/discussion) and the seat work element. In this arrangement, reading is always conducted in a format involving skill instruction, CWPT, and seat work practice. The goal is to increase student engagement with the reading material. CWPT, compared to small reading groups, increases by 20 to 30 times the amount of productive reading time that students might normally receive.

CWPT may also be used to extend reading beyond traditional basal reading texts, to grade level library books, or to topical materials such as social studies or science text books.

SELECT TUTOR/TUTEE PAIRS

In reading CWPT, pair students according to their placement in the same or adjacent reading levels. Tutors do not have written answers. Instead, they detect errors based on their own reading skills. Thus, matching by reading levels is the general rule. Do not expect the tutors to catch all errors tutees make; this is not the primary concern. The main effects of CWPT are derived from the sustained reading practice, and arranging partner reading is the major objective.

However, for one or two lower students, pairing them with peers who are more than one reading level or reader ahead will ensure that a higher percentage of their reading errors are caught and corrected. Having the better reader read first also provides a model for the poorer reader.

If you are using CWPT in reading and spelling, the reading pairing rules should take precedence; that is, pairs for the week are determined by reading ability rather than spelling ability. This arrangement maximizes the accuracy of error correction in all sessions and it keeps pairing and team membership intact for the week.

Select Reading Materials

The reading materials for CWPT oral reading and comprehension are those books being used in the ongoing classroom reading program. This assumes that students have already undergone an initial assessment of their reading skills and have been placed in an appropriate instructional level according to the reading program's guidelines. Accurate instructional placement should result in a student reading 50 to 80% of all words correctly when reading a new passage. If this condition is met, no additional assessment is required. Although these scores may seem low and test a student's frustration level, this would only be the case prior to the beginning of CWPT, during baseline. The reason for having students read at this level prior to tutoring is to make sure that they have room to increase and improve their scores once CWPT in reading has begun. This will ensure that CWPT is an effective learning activity in

that students will have the opportunity to improve their percent correct scores. After tutoring is started, you will need to become concerned with students whose scores continue at a low percentage and review the tutoring procedures and possibly the difficulty level of the text that is being used. Generally, a student reading less than 50% or more than 80% should be placed in new material in order for CWPT to be an appropriate instructional activity. After tutoring has begun, all students should be consistently reading at 80% and higher.

Assign Reading Passages

Coordinate the assignment of CWPT reading passages with each student's reading group assignment. Divide the story into passages of approximately equal length to be used during the four days of CWPT reading sessions. As a general rule, keep passages to a length that allows the lowest reader in each group to read the passage twice in ten minutes. The idea is for the students to practice reading the material by asking, and being asked, comprehension questions. List the reading passages on the **Reading Assignment Form** (Figure 17), which can either be copied and distributed to each tutoring pair, or displayed using an overhead projector.

TRAINING STUDENTS

▶ Distribute Tutoring Materials

1. The basal reading books to be used by students may already be in their desks. If not, they must be available and organized in advance for easy access by all students. If the books

"TOGETHER WE CAN"

READING ASSIGNMENT FORM

WEEK OF: _____11-12_____

READING GROUP: _BARRACUDAS_   READING GROUP: _SHARKS_

DAY	PAGES	ENDING WORD	DAY	PAGES	ENDING WORD
Monday:	24-33	around	Monday:	1-12	know
Tuesday:	34-42	it	Tuesday:	12-13	go
Wednesday:	43-55	them	Wednesday:	26-34	waiting
Thursday:	56-60	low	Thursday:	35-48	tomorrow
Friday:	61-82	time	Friday:	49-76	silence

DAY	PAGES	ENDING WORD	DAY	PAGES	ENDING WORD
Monday:			Monday:		
Tuesday:			Tuesday:		
Wednesday:			Wednesday:		
Thursday:			Friday:		
Friday:			Friday:		

FIGURE 17

Front   Back

FIGURE 18

are to be passed out, make them available in an organized fashion. Some teachers stack books by levels on a table so that helpers can get to the appropriate books quickly. Problems arise if there is not an efficient means for passing out and collecting the books.

2. Deliver or display the **Reading Assignment Forms** to the students so they can determine the pages they are to read.

3. Deliver the **Tutoring Point Sheets** for tutors to record points.

4. Deliver the **Help Card** with the comprehension questions written on the back side (i.e., who, what, when, where, and why) (Figure 18).

► Repeat the Move/Stay procedures discussed in Section 1 to coordinate student teams and pairings. Review these procedures before conducting reading CWPT.

► Awarding Points

1. The tutee begins reading on the first sentence of the passage. The tutee earns two points for each sentence that is read correctly. The tutor marks points on the **Tutoring Point Sheet**, as illustrated in Figures 11 and 12.

2. The tutee earns one point for correctly rereading a sentence after the tutor has detected an error (Figure 19).

3. Students also earn points for answering comprehension questions correctly, as judged by the tutor. The tutor asks the tutee a who, what, when, where, or why question. If it is correct, in the tutor's estimation, the tutee earns two points.

► Correcting Errors

1. When an error occurs during oral reading, the tutor points to the word or words missed in the book

ERROR DEFINITIONS

Substitutions: Saying a word or words in place of the correct word or words.

Omissions: Failure to read a word or words in the sentence.

Additions: Saying a word or words that do not appear in the reading material.

Hesitations: Pausing longer than four seconds during reading.

The Self-Correction Rule: If a student corrects an error on his own within less than four seconds, count the word as correct.

FIGURE 19

and says it correctly, nothing more. The tutee must repeat the word (while looking at it) and then reread the entire sentence.

2. If the tutee rereads the sentence correctly, the tutor interrupts at the end of the sentence and praises the tutee for reading the word correctly. Sample praises are: "Great, Albert, you got it right this time!" or "That was fine—you read 'acorn' correctly!"

3. The tutor then circles one point on the point sheet.

4. The tutee then begins the next sentence.

5. During comprehension, if the tutee does not give the answer that the tutor expected, the tutor says what

he or she thought was the right answer, and why, and asks the question again. When the answer is correct, the tutor awards two points and asks another question.

▶ Earning Bonus Points

During a reading tutoring session, circulate among the students, stop, observe a pair tutoring for 20 to 30 seconds, and award bonus points. Bonus points are given to tutors for maintaining a rapid pace, listening to their partner read, following along in the text, working cooperatively, giving points correctly, using good error correction and modeling of error words, and other positive behaviors such as asking good comprehension questions. One to five bonus points can be awarded to the tutee for "good reading," "trying hard," and "reading so well." Circulating among the students allows you to listen to specific students' oral reading and comprehension and observe how well the tutors are assisting their partner. When you see students who are not carrying out tutoring correctly, review the correct procedures with the pair immediately. At the end of the tutoring sessions, give recognition to the whole class for working hard and doing such a good job of tutoring. Emphasize specific skills for tutoring such as reading along, scoring points, giving quick help with a word, asking great comprehension questions, and giving praise and encouragement to partners.

▶ Teaching CWPT in Reading

Teaching students to play *Together We Can!* in reading follows the same procedure as those described in Section 2, Teaching CWPT. The difference is that you will need to introduce and have your students practice both oral reading tutoring and comprehension tutoring. During oral reading, demonstrate and give examples of errors as described in Figure 19. Have a student begin reading while demonstrating how students earn two points by reading a sentence correctly, and one point when an error is made and is corrected. After the oral reading demonstration, demonstrate the comprehension procedure by asking the student a who, what, when, where, and why question from the prompts listed on the back of the **Help Sign**. These question types are described in Figure 21. Also, let the students know that it is OK to ask the same question over when they cannot think of another "when" question, for example. When you have gone through this sequence one time, demonstrate how the tutor continues to ask who, what, when, etc. questions by making up others, or asking the same question over when one is not immediately apparent. When the students practice, set the timer and have the students practice oral reading, then set it again for a few minutes of comprehension. It helps to write some questions on the board so that when tutors cannot formulate a question, they can use one from the board. When the timer bell rings, have the students reverse roles and practice both the oral reading and comprehension one more time. Subsequently, have the students practice both oral reading and comprehension procedures as above, but add the scoring in both oral reading and comprehension.

Playing *Together We Can!* With Oral Reading

Tutor: "Ok, start on page 32."

Tutee: "The boy went up the hill."

Tutor: "Good, two points."

Tutee: "At the top of the hill he sat down."

Tutor: "Two points!"

Tutee: "He thou. . ." (Hesitation and a pause.)

Tutor: (Pointing to the word) "It's 'thought.'"

Tutee: "Thought."

Tutor: "Right, you got it! Now reread the sentence."

Tutee: "He thought to himself, 'Why am I up here?'"

Tutor: "Good, one point."

When the tutee finishes the passage before the end of the ten-minute session, he or she should reread the passage, continuing to earn points.

Playing *Together We Can!* with Comprehension

After the first ten minute Oral Reading Component is over, the teacher resets the timer, this time for five minutes, and the next phase begins. Here, the tutor's role is to formulate as many comprehension questions over the assigned material as he/she can. Each pair of students will have a **Help Sign** with the words "Who, What, When, Where, and Why" printed on it. When all these types of questions are asked, the vast majority of comprehension skills that the teacher would like

their students to master can be covered. With succeeding grade levels, the types of questions will, of course, become more complex corresponding to reading comprehension objectives. In this case, the prompt sign may be revised to include higher level question cues. If the tutor cannot think up a new question, the student can simply look at this card for help with an idea for another question or repeat a previously asked question. If a student really gets stuck, the **Help Sign** can be used for teacher assistance.

▶ Reporting Points

The total points for reading and comprehension are reported at the end of the tutoring session just as they were for spelling and math. Weekly winning teams in reading are the team with the highest point total. Record the points on the **Team Point Chart**, and acknowledge and applaud the winning and losing teams. Remember to praise students who are good sports.

EVALUATING READING CWPT

MATERIALS NEEDED FOR EACH STUDENT

► Two reading **Student Assessment Sheets**—one for pre and one for post,

► **Reading Rate Chart**,

► Stopwatch

SELECT TARGET STUDENTS

As in spelling and math, targeted students are given a pre and post oral reading rate check and comprehension questions once per week. The pre and post student assessments, as in spelling, are completed at the same time. As in Figure 16, **Weekly Time Required**, this will generally occur on Friday or day 5 of the chart. The pre student assessment is based on a passage that will be covered during the next week. Using the **Reading Assignment Form** (Figure 17) select a passage that you are sure the student will be tutored on the next week. The passage that has been planned for the next Thursday is the best one for assessment.

The post student assessment is based upon material that was tutored on previous days during the current week. Generally, this will be the passage the student had on Thursday (Day 4) of the week. If tutoring was not held that day, then select Wednesday or another previous day. The rule is to select a passage that the student was tutored on the school day before the **Student Assessment Sheet** is completed.

In contrast to spelling and math where **all** students are assessed (i.e., weekly post tests), CWPT with reading is based upon selecting five students for weekly assessment. These five students will remain the same over the coming weeks of the program. Because it is generally difficult for most teachers to assess every student in their classroom (e.g., listen to more than 20 students read individually each week), we have found that selecting five students for assessment can be fairly representative of how the whole class is performing. Obviously, the more students selected, the better the representation will be. If at all possible, assessments with every student in the class would be ideal. However, because of time constraints for most teachers, five students are considered to be a minimum.

When selecting the five students, choose the three lowest readers (your assessment) and two students who would be at the middle of the class in reading skills (again, your assessment). For the three students with low reading skills, give priority to any that participate in the Special Education Program and are also the lowest readers of your class. The main idea when selecting the five students is to have a group that is fairly representative of "low" and "average" skill levels in your class. That way, students who are targeted for assessment provide a fairly good estimate as to the effects of the program on other students in their similar ability group. With the minimum of five, you need to be able to assume that if the three "lows" are making progress, as are the two "averages," then the other students in the class, including "average" and especially "highs," are also doing well. Oftentimes, this assumption can be bolstered by your close observation of other children during the CWPT sessions and how well they seem to be doing with reading and comprehension in relation to others.

▶ Check Reading Rate

During the oral reading assessment, it is important to gain a "pure" score of the student's reading rate skill. Here it is important to allow the student to read with little or no help from the teacher. Obviously, interruptions such as phonics questions, being asked to repeat a word or phrase, being stopped and corrected on a word, take away from the student's oral reading rate score. Before starting, tell the student where to begin reading and how far to go in the passage. Let them know that you will not be able to help them and, if they come to a word they don't know, skip it and go on reading. After the student begins reading, you will need to record errors on the **Student Assessment Sheet** (Figure 20). If a student cannot figure out a word, but keeps trying, prompt them to "skip it and go on to the next." If the student comes to a word and stops, allow about four seconds, and then prompt the student to "go on to the next word." If the student completes the passage prior to one minute, prompt the student to go back to the beginning and start over. Words in the pas-

sage that are reread by the student during the one-minute rate check are added to the **Total Words Read** on the **Student Assessment Sheet**. Immediately after the child has read, complete the comprehension assessment by asking the student five questions based on the reading passage. Determine if the responses are correct based upon your own judgment.

The following describes how to conduct the reading rate checks.

1. Call one of the target students up to your desk to read to you orally for one minute.

2. Instruct the student to locate the previously tutored passage in his or her book.

"TOGETHER WE CAN"

STUDENT ASSESSMENT SHEET

Pre test: _____   Post test: _____

Teacher: _Mayer_   Student: _J.D. Smith_

Reading Textbook: _Dolphins_   Week of: _Sept. 7, 1994_

1 - Minute Oral Reading Measure:

Begin: Page: _59_   Words: _Many_   Words: _____
End: Page: _60_   Words: _happy_   Words: _____

1	2	3	4	5	6	7	8	9	10
11	12	13	14	15	16	17	18	19	20
21	22	23	24	25	26	27	28	29	30

Total Words Read: _150_
Total Errors: (EWPM) _− 5_
Total Correct Words: (CWPM) _145_

Comprehension Measure: Correct/Incorrect
                                         + or −
1. Who   [+]
2. What   [+]
3. When   [+]
4. Where   [+]
5. Why   [−]

correct x 20% = _80_ % Correct

Teacher Comments: _Only three tutoring sessions._

| Mon _+_ | Tues _+_ | Wed _0_ | Thurs _+_ | Fri _−_ |
| (+) Student Tutored | (−) Student Not Tutored | (0) Student Absent | | |

FIGURE 20

3. Record the beginning page and word on the **Student Assessment Sheet.**

4. Start the stopwatch and instruct the student to begin reading.

5. Record each error the student makes on the **Student Assessment Sheet** (see Figure 20) by marking the next item to the right in the error tally section of the sheet.

6. Stop the student at exactly one minute. Record the page number and last word said by the student.

7. Count the total number of words from the book or passage that the student read orally. (Do this after the student has completed the comprehension check.)

8. Check the student's reading comprehension and then do the calculations.

DEFINITIONS OF COMPREHENSION QUESTIONS

QUESTION TYPES	DESCRIPTION
1. Who	Ask for a specific character. **Example:** Who did the little girl want to visit?
2. What	Ask for word meaning. Ask about specific story events. Ask about the sequence of events. Ask about the main idea. **Examples:** What does "horizon" mean? What happened when the girl visited her Grandfather? What were all the things they did after they went to the park? What was the story about?
3. Where	Ask about location. **Examples:** Where did Granddad find his keys? Where was the park?
4. When	Ask about sequence of events. Ask about the time of specific story events. **Examples:** When did Granddad decide to push the girl in the swing? When did Grandmother whisper in Granddad's ear?
5. Why	Ask about specific story events. Ask students to make inferences about story events. **Examples:** Why do you think Granddad said, at first, that they couldn't go to the park? Why did Granddad smile after Grandmother whispered in his ear?

FIGURE 21

CHECK COMPREHENSION

After the reading rate check has been completed for each target student, ask questions related to the student's comprehension of the material read using the **Student Assessment Sheet**. The teacher should ask who, what, where, when, and why questions based on the passage. The definitions of these categories (Figure 21) coincide with the typical types of comprehension most asked by reading teachers.

One question of each type can be asked and scored as correct (+) or incorrect (–) by the teacher. This measure provides the teacher with a percent correct score and feedback on the student's understanding of what was read during the reading rate check session (see Figure 20).

After completing the **Student Assessment Sheet**, repeat the testing process (reading rate and comprehension) with the next target student.

MONITOR STUDENT PROGRESS

Monitor progress for the five (or more) target students. Record the correct, the incorrect rate, and the comprehension scores weekly on the **Reading Rate Chart** (Figure 22) to determine reading progress over time. Prepare one chart for each student you are monitoring. Post these graphs on the wall near the other CWPT charts and materials so you can refer to them and bring them to the attention of the students. Students can then see their growth in reading (see Figure 22).

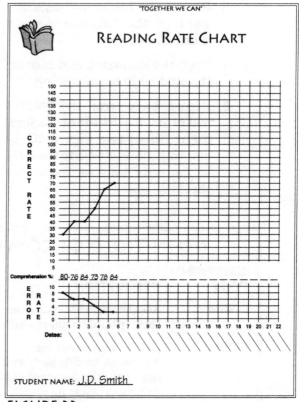

FIGURE 22

TROUBLESHOOTING

TROUBLESHOOTING

I'm not getting the academic gains I want.

▶ 1. Make sure you schedule a time that will allow tutoring to occur every day for the full time limit. If possible, conduct the tutoring sessions at the same time every day.

2. Arrange tutoring during a time period when all students are present (avoid periods when students are out for special lab times or activity sessions). Research shows that students who miss even one day of tutoring per week will not perform their best on the posttest.

3. Avoid scheduling conflicts with outside activities such as assemblies, field trips, etc.

4. Make certain the material tutored each week is appropriate and challenging. Research shows it is common for teachers to give students material that is too easy. Thus, too many students do not gain.

5. Make certain tutors are following the procedures correctly. For example, if the error correction procedures are not used, gains will not follow.

6. Make certain students are covering the material twice in ten minutes—if not, cut length so practice can occur.

What about students who cheat by marking more points than earned and saying they are bonus points?

▶ When awarding bonus points, use a different colored marker than the one used by the tutor so that the number of bonus points is evident.

What about the tutor who cheats by merely marking more points than the tutee earns?

▶ From the beginning of the program, you must ensure that students use the points correctly. Monitor each session to prevent cheating. Teach the students that the number of points they earn is related to the amount of work they have completed. For example, the number of words spelled and corrected in spelling on the tutee's worksheet should sum to the number on the student's **Tutoring Point Sheet**. Pick a student at random each day and perform this check aloud and publicly so that all students learn that you will be monitoring their efforts. Students whose point totals are not within five or ten points of the correct amount should lose their points for the day. Also, award bonus points during tutoring for the correct use of points by the tutor.

Watch the **Team Point Chart** to see if any students show large jumps in point totals. A gain of 20 points is laudatory, but a gain of 50 points is certainly suspicious. These monitoring checks, with feedback to students, prevent the students from reporting unearned points. Let the students know you are on top of this. Do not tolerate grossly inaccurate point totals. This will ruin the program.

What about slower students (e.g., students who don't write as quickly or who are perfectionists, etc.) who never get to practice the last word or problem in the list?

► 1. To provide students with practice on all the items on the tutoring list during the week, have the tutors begin at the bottom of the list and work from the bottom up on alternate days of tutoring.

2. Consider shortening the list for your slowest students.

3. Motivate perfectionists to respond faster by providing a special reinforcer for point-earning improvements.

I have an uneven number of students. How do I use CWPT and have the point assignment be fair?

► Whenever an odd number of students exists on a team, form a triad (three students). In this situation, one student tutors two tutees at the same time. One student in the triad will have a double opportunity to earn points, because the student will have been the tutee twice. In order to prevent the team with a triad from winning because of this double opportunity, have this student report the highest number of points he or she earned in one of the ten-minute sessions. Triads are always composed of students on the same team.

After the excitement of playing Together We Can! it's hard to get my students to transition to the next activity.

► After the excitement of tutoring, students need a clear transition back into the regular classroom routine. In such instances, a signal that the tutoring period is over can be helpful.

Here is an example of a transition routine:

Turn the classroom lights off. This signal is for students to put their heads on their desks. Have the student helpers collect tutoring materials.

Quietly tell the students that you want them to look at you when the lights come back on. Then turn on the lights.

Now begin the next activity.

What about students who are loud, disruptive, or off task before, during, and after the CWPT exercise?

▲There are several reasons for this. First, CWPT is often one of the few classroom instructional activities that permits students to speak to and interact with their classmates. In addition, CWPT contains several components (e.g., points, team competition, etc.) that generate enthusiasm and excitement from the students and that may turn into excessively loud or disruptive classroom behavior. Therefore, our first recommendation is that you establish a set of classroom rules that clearly specify your expectations to the students. Experience shows that the problem of loud, disruptive, or off-task student behavior is most prevalent during the transition periods when students are required to move to their tutoring partners or report their point totals to the teacher. Therefore, a list of CWPT rules might include the following:

1. Students talk only during the actual tutoring process and not during the other periods of the game (e.g., moving or point reporting periods).

2. Students talk to their tutoring partner only and should not speak with other students in the classroom.

3. Students talk about tutoring only and should discuss other topics at recess time.

4. Students keep their voices at low levels throughout the tutoring activity.

Although rules such as these are helpful, their mere presence will probably not prevent students from exhibiting some inappropriate behaviors. You must routinely enforce these classroom rules; you should monitor the students' behavior throughout the tutoring period and provide various consequences both when students follow the rules (e.g., teacher awards bonus points) and when they disregard the rules (e.g., teacher deducts bonus points).

Another factor contributing to this problem is the manner in which instructions are given to the students and the degree to which students comply. A very structured approach that is clear and that leads all students to the goal of the instruction is best. Figure 23 shows how this procedure should be conducted. The purpose of this procedure is to tell them what to do, check their comprehension, and then give a clear signal when they are to do it. This structured approach of (1) instruct; (2) query for comprehension; (3) signal to go; and (4) praise correct execution of the command is very effective in solving problems of group compliance during transitions into and out of tutoring.

SAMPLE INSTRUCTION

Teacher: "Everyone look at me. Good, Gwen is looking. Bill is looking. Now everyone is looking." (Teacher observes and praises students for executing the instruction. Teacher does not go on until all students are looking.)

Teacher: "We are going to begin tutoring now. What are we going to do?"

Students: "Start tutoring!"

Teacher: "Right!"

Teacher prepares the students for the next step and queries for their comprehension.

Teacher: "When I say go, please move and stand by your partners. What will you do?"

Students: "Move and stand by our partners."

Teacher: "When will you do it?"

Students: "When you say go!"

Teachers: "Right. Ok, go."

FIGURE 23

*T*oo much time is being wasted on noninstructional activities such as moving to tutoring partners and reporting points. How can I keep to the 25- to 30-minute session time frame?

▶Delays may be avoided by using the timer to set minimum time limits. Provide the class with a reasonable duration of time to complete designated tasks, and then provide positive consequences to those students or team(s) who meet these time limits. Bonus points or special activities often make ideal reinforcers for successful students. Those students failing to meet the time limit have simply lost the opportunity to earn additional points or activities.

One word of caution relates to the specific time limits that you impose upon the students: Determine these time limits carefully. For example, if a second grade class consistently requires seven minutes to move and prepare for tutoring, do not impose a time limit of four minutes because this would probably lead to more failure and frustration for both you and the students. A more appropriate goal for the first several days might be six minutes, and then five, etc. When used in this gradually adjusting manner, the "timer procedure" is likely to be successful.

W̲hat do I do about those students who do not follow the tutoring procedure correctly? Some tutors are lax in checking the tutees responses, some don't require three practice trials, etc.

▲Two comments are appropriate before discussing strategies to remediate this problem. First, only a few students (e.g., three to four per classroom) generally exhibit these behaviors often enough to present a problem for you. Second, these students are considered problematic because they may cause a drop in performance on posttests or rate checks as a consequence. The following strategy pertains to maintaining high quality tutoring and it applies to all students:

You must monitor and provide bonus points for correct tutoring behaviors. You must supervise students' responding in order to achieve a successful program. If you walk around the classroom, monitoring tutoring behaviors by providing praise, giving bonus points and correction, and answering students' questions, you will reduce the number of problems and prevent future problems.

Some teachers enjoy their new role of supervising students responding in CWPT this way. Others would rather correct papers at their desk and let the tutors handle CWPT. Ultimately, the trade-off is simple: Those who complete these tasks consistently and conscientiously will experience fewer problems, and both you and your students will obtain greater benefits from the program.

Appendix

RESEARCH ON CLASSWIDE PEER TUTORING

Study I

Study I is a summary of the effects of a four-year longitudinal study of the academic benefits of ClassWide Peer Tutoring (CWPT) (Greenwood, Delquadri, & Hall, 1989). For an experimental group of low socioeconomic students (SES) in four schools, teachers employed CWPT in first, second, third, and fourth grades. Their results were compared to an equivalent control group of low socioeconomic students (two schools) and a high socioeconomic control group (three schools) whose teachers employed conventional instructional methods. The students in the CWPT group made significant gains on the Reading, Mathematics, and Language subtest scales of the Metropolitan Achievement Test (MAT). The means data for each subtest is presented for each group. The post adjusted means reflect posttest differences between the groups after being equated statistically on their first grade pretest scores and IQ scores. These adjusted means reflect a "fair" comparison of achievement patterns between these groups (Figure 24).

At the end of fourth grade, the students in the experimental group exceeded students in the control group by 10 (reading) to 13 (language) percentile points, whereas the high socioeconomic comparison group was 16 (math) to 22 (reading) percentiles above the control group. The students in the experimental group ended fourth grade at the 44th percentile in reading, 50th percentile in math, and 54th percentile in language. The national median on the test is the 50th percentile. In each area, the students in the experimental group approached or exceeded this level. The same percentiles for the students in the low SES control group were the 34th in reading, 43rd in math, and 42nd in language.

STUDY I

METROPOLITAN ACHIEVEMENT TEST MEANS SUMMARY

LANGUAGE		FALL 1ST GRADE	SPRING 4TH GRADE	
Low Socioeconomic CWPT Intervention	Normal Curve Equivalent Grade Equivalent	39.2 0.7	53.9 5.9	
				***
Low Socioeconomic Control Group	Normal Curve Equivalent Grade Equivalent	39.4 0.7	42.2 4.5	
				ttt
High Socioeconomic Control Group	Normal Curve Equivalent Grade Equivalent	52.2 1.1	53.9 5.9	
MATH				
Low Socioeconomic CWPT Intervention	Normal Curve Equivalent Grade Equivalent	42.2 0.8	49.5 4.9	
				*
Low Socioeconomic Control Group	Normal Curve Equivalent Grade Equivalent	42.1 0.8	42.6 4.4	
				tt
High Socioeconomic Control Group	Normal Curve Equivalent Grade Equivalent	53.4 1.3	53.5 5.4	
READING				
Low Socioeconomic CWPT Intervention	Normal Curve Equivalent Grade Equivalent	50.1 1.1	44.0 4.4	
				**
Low Socioeconomic Control Group	Normal Curve Equivalent Grade Equivalent	44.0 0.9	34.2 3.6	
				ttt
High Socioeconomic Control Group	Normal Curve Equivalent Grade Equivalent	57.8 1.2	50.3 5.4	

* = Comparison between low SES students who did and did not receive CWPT where
* = p <.05, ** = p <.01, *** = p <.001
= Comparison between low SES students who did and did not receive CWPT where
t = p <.05, tt = p <.01, ttt = p <.001

FIGURE 24

Study II

Study II is a summary of the effects of a three-year longitudinal study of the academic benefits of CWPT. This study had two control groups (Low SES and High SES) and two CWPT groups. Although the CWPT groups were trained in the correct procedures, some teachers did not implement CWPT as instructed. This Low Implementation group was compared to a High Implementation CWPT group.

The results shown in the following graphs show that the High Implementation CWPT group was at grade level at the end of third grade (3.9). As expected, the High SES group was above grade level. The important point in this study is the similarity between the Low Implementation CWPT group and the control group; the results of the two groups are almost the same. Simply stated, if you want results, you have to follow the directions in this manual (Figure 25).

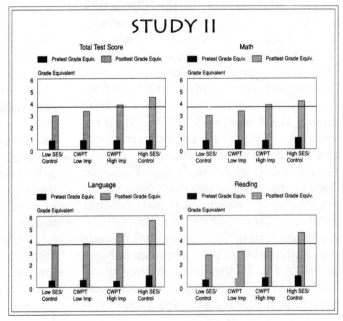

FIGURE 25

REFERENCES

Some of the research that supports the classwide peer tutoring concept can be found in the following sources:

Delquadri, J., Greenwood, C.R., Stretton, K., & Hall, R.V. (1983). The peer tutoring spelling game: A classroom procedure for increasing opportunity to respond and spelling performance. *Education and Treatment of Children, 6,* 225-239.

Greenwood, C.R. (1991). Longitudinal analysis of time, engagement, and achievement of at-risk versus non-risk students. *Exceptional Children, 57*(6), 521-535.

Greenwood, C.R., Carta, J.J., & Hall, R.V. (1988). The use of peer tutoring strategies in classroom management and educational instruction. *School Psychological Review, 17,* 258-275.

Greenwood, C.R. & Delquadri, J. (1995). Classwide peer tutoring and the prevention of school failure. *Preventing School Failure, 39,* 21-25.

Greenwood, C.R., Delquadri, J., & Hall, R.V. (1989). Longitudinal effects of classwide peer tutoring. *Journal of Educational Psychology, 81,* 371-383.

Greenwood, C.R., Dinwiddie, G., Terry, B., Wade, L., Standley, S., Thibadeau, S., & Delquadri, J. (1984). Teacher-versus peer-mediated instruction: An eco-behavioral analysis of achievement outcomes. *Journal of Applied Behavior Analysis, 17,* 521-538.

Greenwood, C.R., Finney, R., Terry, B., Arreaga-Mayer, C., Carta, J.J., Delquadri, J., & Walker, D. (1993). Monitoring, improving, and maintaining quality implementation of the classwide peer tutoring program using behavioral and computer technology. *Education and Treatment of Children, 16*(1), 19-47.

Greenwood, C.R., Maheady, L., & Carta, J.J. (1991). Peer tutoring programs in the regular education classroom. In G. Stoner, M.R. Shinn, & H.M. Walker (Eds.), *Interventions for achievement and behavior problems* (pp. 179-200). Washington, DC: National Association for School Psychologists (NASP).

Greenwood, C.R., Terry, B., Arreaga-Mayer, C., & Finney, R. (1992). The classwide peer tutoring program: Implementation factors moderating students' achievement. Special issue: The education crisis: Issues, perspectives, solutions. *Journal of Applied Behavior Analysis, 25*(1), 101-116.

Greenwood, C.R., Terry, B., Utley, C.A., Montagna, D., & Walker, D. (1993). Achievement, placement, and services: Middle school benefits of classwide peer tutoring used at the elementary school. *School Psychology Review, 22*(3), 497-516.

Harper, G.F., Mallette, B., Maheady, L., Bentley, A.E., & Moore, J. (1995). Retention and treatment failure in classwide peer tutoring: Implications for further research. *Journal of Behavioral Education, 5,* 399-414.

► APPENDIX

Harper, G.F., Mallette, B., Maheady, L., Parkes, V., & Moore, J. (1993). Retention and generalization of spelling words acquired using peer-mediated instructional procedure by children with mild handicapping conditions. *Journal of Behavioral Education, 3*(1), 25-38.

Maheady, L. & Harper, G. (1987). A classwide peer tutoring program to improve the spelling performance of low-income, third-, and fourth-grade students. *Education and Treatment of Children, 10,* 120-133.

Utley, C.A., Mortweet, S.L., & Greenwood, C.R. (1997). Peer-mediated instruction and interventions. *Focus on Exceptional children, 29*(5), 1-23.

REPRODUCIBLE
MASTERS

Items marked with (L) will work best if you laminate them.

Monthly Subject List
Weekly Tutoring List
Percentage Conversion Chart (L)
Happy Gram
Good Sports Handout
Tutoring Worksheet
Tutoring Point Sheet (L)
Help Sign (L) (Help on one side; "who," "what," "when,"
     "where," "why" on the other)
Bonus Points Reminder Chart
Reading Assignment Form
Student Assessment Sheet
Reading Rate Chart

These items are provided as 20" x 30" laminated posters:

Teams and Partners Chart
Pretest/Posttest Score Chart
Team Point Charts (2 provided—1 for each team)

Note: Please use only dry erase markers on these posters.

"TOGETHER WE CAN!"
MONTHLY SUBJECT LIST

TEACHER: _____ MONTH: _____ SUBJECT: _____

	WEEK 1: MONDAY DATE __/__/__	WEEK 2: MONDAY DATE __/__/__	WEEK 3: MONDAY DATE __/__/__	WEEK 4: MONDAY DATE __/__/__
1.				
2.				
3.				
4.				
5.				
6.				
7.				
8.				
9.				
10.				
11.				
12.				
13.				
14.				
15.				
16.				
17.				
18.				
19.				
20.				
21.				
22.				
23.				
24.				
25.				
26.				
27.				
28.				
29.				
30.				

© Copyright by Greenwood, Delquadri, and Carta, 1997. All rights reserved.

© Copyright by Crestwood, Delmar and Obex, 1992. All rights reserved.

WEEKLY TUTORING LIST

TEACHER: _____ MONTH: _____ SUBJECT: _____

1. _____	29. _____
2. _____	30. _____
3. _____	31. _____
4. _____	32. _____
5. _____	33. _____
6. _____	34. _____
7. _____	35. _____
8. _____	36. _____
9. _____	37. _____
10. _____	38. _____
11. _____	39. _____
12. _____	40. _____
13. _____	41. _____
14. _____	42. _____
15. _____	43. _____
16. _____	44. _____
17. _____	45. _____
18. _____	46. _____
19. _____	47. _____
20. _____	48. _____
21. _____	49. _____
22. _____	50. _____
23. _____	51. _____
24. _____	52. _____
25. _____	53. _____
26. _____	54. _____
27. _____	55. _____
28. _____	56. _____

© Copyright by Greenwood, Delquadri, and Carta, 1997. All rights reserved.

"TOGETHER WE CAN!"
PERCENTAGE CONVERSION CHART

NUMBER OF PROBLEMS CORRECT

NUMBER OF PROBLEMS	0	1	2	3	4	5	6	7	8	9	10	11	12	13	14	15	16	17	18	19	20	21	22	23	24	25	26	27	28	29	30
1	0	100																													
2	0	50	100																												
3	0	33	67	100																											
4	0	25	50	75	100																										
5	0	20	40	60	80	100																									
6	0	17	33	50	67	83	100																								
7	0	14	26	42	57	71	86	100																							
8	0	13	25	36	50	63	75	86	100																						
9	0	11	22	33	44	56	67	78	89	100																					
10	0	10	20	30	40	50	60	70	80	90	100																				
11	0	9	18	27	36	45	55	64	73	82	91	100																			
12	0	8	17	25	33	42	50	58	67	75	83	92	100																		
13	0	8	15	23	31	36	46	54	62	69	77	85	92	100																	
14	0	7	14	21	29	36	43	50	57	64	71	79	86	93	100																
15	0	7	13	20	27	33	40	47	53	60	67	73	80	87	93	100															
16	0	6	13	19	25	31	36	44	50	56	63	69	75	81	86	94	100														
17	0	6	12	18	24	29	35	41	47	53	59	65	71	76	82	88	94	100													
18	0	6	11	17	22	28	33	39	44	50	56	61	67	72	78	83	89	94	100												
19	0	5	11	16	21	26	32	37	42	47	53	58	63	68	74	79	84	89	95	100											
20	0	5	10	15	20	25	30	36	40	45	50	55	60	65	70	75	80	85	90	95	100										
21	0	5	10	14	19	24	29	33	38	43	48	52	57	62	67	71	76	81	86	90	95	100									
22	0	5	9	14	18	23	27	32	36	41	45	50	55	59	64	68	73	77	82	86	91	95	100								
23	0	4	9	13	18	22	26	30	35	39	43	48	52	57	61	65	70	74	78	83	87	91	96	100							
24	0	4	8	13	17	21	25	29	33	36	42	46	50	54	58	63	67	71	75	79	83	88	92	96	100						
25	0	4	8	12	16	20	24	24	28	36	40	44	48	52	56	60	64	68	72	76	80	84	88	92	96	100					
26	0	4	8	12	15	19	23	27	31	35	38	42	46	50	54	58	62	65	69	73	77	81	85	88	92	96	100				
27	0	4	7	11	15	19	22	26	30	33	37	41	44	48	52	56	59	63	67	70	74	78	81	85	89	93	96	100			
28	0	4	7	11	14	18	21	25	29	32	36	39	43	46	50	54	57	61	64	68	71	75	79	82	86	89	93	97	100		
29	0	3	7	10	14	17	21	24	26	31	34	38	41	45	48	52	55	59	62	66	70	72	76	79	83	86	90	93	97	100	
30	0	3	7	10	13	17	20	23	27	30	33	37	40	43	47	50	53	57	60	63	67	70	73	77	80	83	87	90	93	97	100

Divide the number of problems correct by the number of problems.
Move the decimal two places to the right and round up.

© Copyright by Greenwood, Delquadri, and Carta, 1997. All rights reserved.

HAPPY GRAM

Super Week Award!!

This is to certify that

_____
STUDENT'S NAME

has shown improvement in

_____ *this week.*

_____   _____
DATE   TEACHER'S NAME

HAPPY GRAM

Super Week Award!!

This is to certify that

_____
STUDENT'S NAME

has shown improvement in

_____ *this week.*

_____   _____
DATE   TEACHER'S NAME

© Copyright by Greenwood, Delquadri, and Carta, 1997. All rights reserved.

WIN/LOSE

GOOD SPORTS

Praise the winners for their accomplishment

Praise the effort of the losing team

Don't tease the losers

Don't cry or complain about losing

Know they will have a new chance to win on another day

© Copyright by Greenwood, Delquadri, and Carta, 1997. All rights reserved.

"TOGETHER WE CAN!"
TUTORING WORKSHEET

STUDENT: _____ DATE: _____ SUBJECT: _____

	CORRECTION PRACTICE		
	1	**2**	**3**
1.			
2.			
3.			
4.			
5.			
6.			
7.			
8.			
9.			
10.			
11.			
12.			
13.			
14.			
15.			
16.			
17.			
18.			
19.			
20.			
21.			
22.			
23.			
24.			
25.			
26.			
27.			
28.			
29.			
30.			

© Copyright by Greenwood, Delquadri, and Carta, 1997. All rights reserved.

"TOGETHER WE CAN!"
TUTORING POINT SHEET

STUDENT: _____   DATE: _____   SUBJECT: _____

TIMES THROUGH: 1 2 3 4 5 6 7 8 9 10

1	2	3	4	5	6	7	8	9	10	11	12
13	14	15	16	17	18	19	20	21	22	23	24
25	26	27	28	29	30	31	32	33	34	35	36
37	38	39	40	41	42	43	44	45	46	47	48
49	50	51	52	53	54	55	56	57	58	59	60
61	62	63	64	65	66	67	68	69	70	71	72
73	74	75	76	77	78	79	80	81	82	83	84
85	86	87	88	89	90	91	92	93	94	95	96
97	98	99	100	101	102	103	104	105	106	107	108
109	110	111	112	113	114	115	116	117	118	119	120
121	122	123	124	125	126	127	128	129	130	131	132
133	134	135	136	137	138	139	140	141	142	143	144
145	146	147	148	149	150	151	152	153	154	155	156
157	158	159	160	161	162	163	164	165	166	167	168
169	170	171	172	173	174	175	176	177	178	179	180
181	182	183	184	185	186	187	188	189	190	191	192
193	194	195	196	197	198	199	200	201	202	203	204
205	206	207	208	209	210	211	212	213	214	215	216
217	218	219	220	221	222	223	224	225	226	227	228
229	230	231	232	233	234	235	236	237	238	239	240
241	242	243	244	245	246	247	248	249	250	251	252
253	254	255	256	257	258	259	260	261	262	263	264
265	266	267	268	269	270	271	272	273	274	275	276
277	278	279	280	281	282	283	284	285	286	287	288
289	290	291	292	293	294	295	296	297	298	299	300
301	302	303	304	305	306	307	308	309	310	311	312
313	314	315	316	317	318	319	320	321	322	323	324
325	326	327	328	329	330	331	332	333	334	335	336
337	338	339	340	341	342	343	344	345	346	347	348
349	350	351	352	353	354	355	356	357	358	359	360
361	362	363	364	365	366	367	368	369	370	371	372
373	374	375	376	377	378	379	380	381	382	383	384

© Copyright by Greenwood, Delquadri, and Carta, 1997. All rights reserved.

385	386	387	388	389	390	391	392	393	394	395	396
397	398	399	400	401	402	403	404	405	406	407	408
409	410	411	412	413	414	415	416	417	418	419	420
421	422	423	424	425	426	427	428	429	430	431	432
433	434	435	436	437	438	439	440	441	442	443	444
445	446	447	448	449	450	451	452	453	454	455	456
457	458	459	460	461	462	463	464	465	466	467	468
469	470	471	472	473	474	475	476	477	478	479	480
481	482	483	484	485	486	487	488	489	490	491	492
493	494	495	496	497	498	499	500	501	502	503	504
505	506	507	508	509	510	511	512	513	514	515	516
517	518	519	520	521	522	523	524	525	526	527	528
529	530	531	532	533	534	535	536	537	538	539	540
541	542	543	544	545	546	547	548	549	550	551	552
553	554	555	556	557	558	559	560	561	562	563	564
565	566	567	568	569	570	571	572	573	574	575	576
577	578	579	580	581	582	583	584	585	586	587	588
589	590	591	592	593	594	595	596	597	598	599	600
601	602	603	604	605	606	607	608	609	610	611	612
613	614	615	616	617	618	619	620	621	622	623	624
625	626	627	628	629	630	631	632	633	634	635	636
637	638	639	640	641	642	643	644	645	646	647	648
649	650	651	652	653	654	655	656	657	658	659	660
661	662	663	664	665	666	667	668	669	670	671	672
673	674	675	676	677	678	679	680	681	682	683	684
685	686	687	688	689	690	691	692	693	694	695	696
697	698	699	700	701	702	703	704	705	706	707	708
709	710	711	712	713	714	715	716	717	718	719	720
721	722	723	724	725	726	727	728	729	730	731	732
733	734	735	736	737	738	739	740	741	742	743	744
745	746	747	748	749	750	751	752	753	754	755	756
757	758	759	760	761	762	763	764	765	766	767	768
769	770	771	772	773	774	775	776	777	778	779	780
781	782	783	784	785	786	787	788	789	790	791	792
793	794	795	796	797	798	799	800	801	802	803	804

© Copyright by Greenwood, Delquadri, and Carta, 1997. All rights reserved.

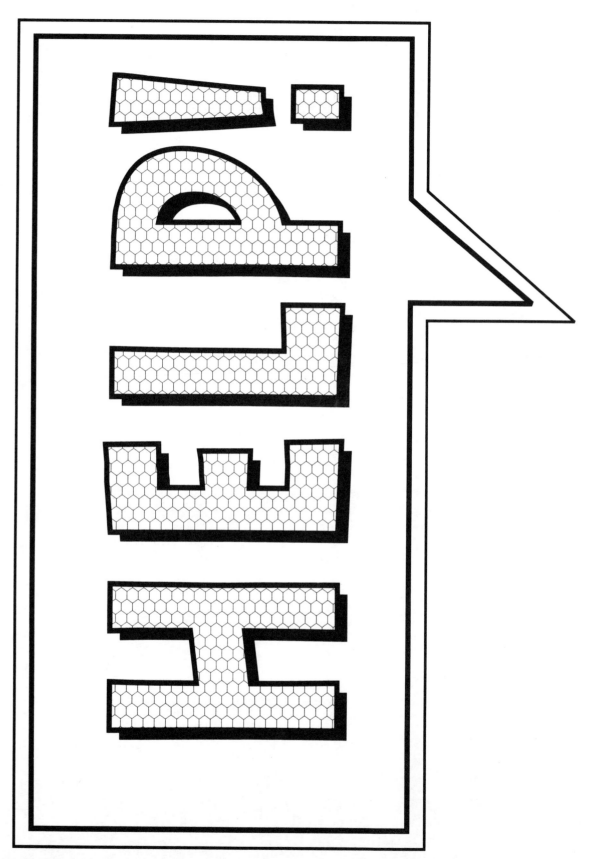

© Copyright by Greenwood, Delquadri, and Carta, 1997. All rights reserved.

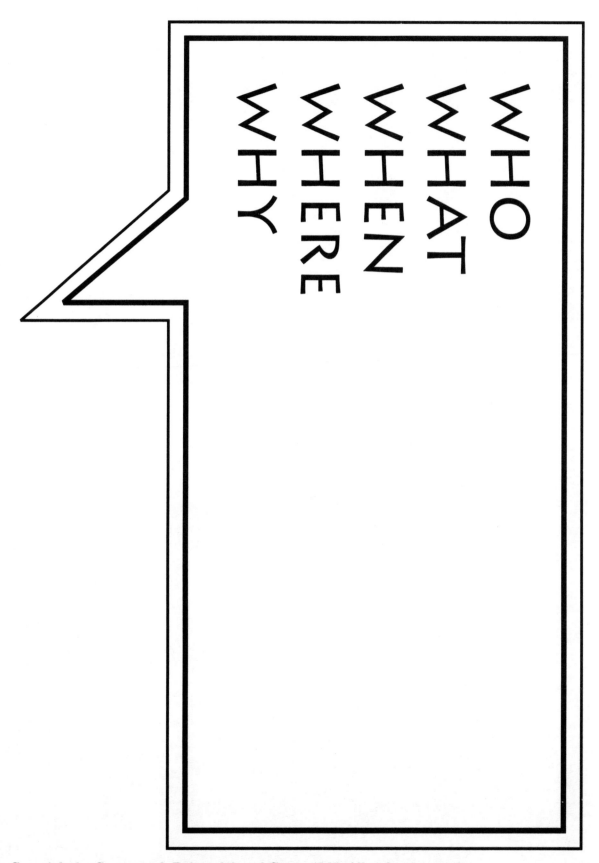

© Copyright by Greenwood, Delquadri, and Carta, 1997. All rights reserved.

"TOGETHER WE CAN!"

BONUS POINTS REMINDER CHART

Tutors can earn 1–5 bonus points by:

Reading words clearly to your tutee

Watching your tutee write words

Correcting tutee's mistakes

Giving the right number of points to the tutee

Moving quickly and quietly to your partner

Keeping the tutee busy

Tutees can earn 1–5 bonus points by:

Writing quickly

Saying and writing words at the same time

Writing answers three times after a mistake

Putting pencil down when the timer rings

© Copyright by Greenwood, Delquadri, and Carta, 1997. All rights reserved.

"TOGETHER WE CAN!"
READING ASSIGNMENT FORM

WEEK OF: _____

READING GROUP: _____   **READING GROUP:** _____

DAY	PAGES	ENDING WORD
Monday:	_____	_____
Tuesday:	_____	_____
Wednesday:	_____	_____
Thursday:	_____	_____
Friday:	_____	_____

DAY	PAGES	ENDING WORD
Monday:	_____	_____
Tuesday:	_____	_____
Wednesday:	_____	_____
Thursday:	_____	_____
Friday:	_____	_____

DAY	PAGES	ENDING WORD
Monday:	_____	_____
Tuesday:	_____	_____
Wednesday:	_____	_____
Thursday:	_____	_____
Friday:	_____	_____

DAY	PAGES	ENDING WORD
Monday:	_____	_____
Tuesday:	_____	_____
Wednesday:	_____	_____
Thursday:	_____	_____
Friday:	_____	_____

© Copyright by Greenwood, Delquadri, and Carta, 1997. All rights reserved.

TOGETHER WE CAN

READING
ASSIGNMENT FORM

WEEK OF:

READING
GROUP:

READING
GROUP:

DAY	PAGES	WORD	ENDING	DAY	PAGES	WORD	ENDING
Monday				Monday			
Tuesday				Tuesday			
Wednesday				Wednesday			
Thursday				Thursday			
Friday				Friday			

DAY	PAGES	WORD	ENDING	DAY	PAGES	WORD	ENDING
Monday				Monday			
Tuesday				Tuesday			
Wednesday				Wednesday			
Thursday				Thursday			
Friday				Friday			

Copyright by Greenwood, Delmarva and Parts, 1997. All rights reserved.

"TOGETHER WE CAN!"

STUDENT ASSESSMENT SHEET

Pre test: _____   Post test: _____

Teacher: _____   Student: _____

Reading Textbook: _____   Week of: _____

1 - Minute Oral Reading Measure:

Begin: Page: _____   Words: _____   Words: _____

End: Page: _____   Words: _____   Words: _____

1	2	3	4	5	6	7	8	9	10
11	12	13	14	15	16	17	18	19	20
21	22	23	24	25	26	27	28	29	30

Total Words Read: _____

Total Errors: (EWPM) _____

Total Correct Words: (CWPM) _____

Comprehension Measure: Correct/Incorrect
                                                + or –

1. Who   [   ]

2. What   [   ]

3. When   [   ]

4. Where   [   ]

5. Why   [   ]

correct x 20% = _____ % Correct

Teacher Comments: _____

_____

Mon _____	Tues _____	Wed _____	Thurs _____	Fri _____
(+) Student Tutored		(–) Student Not Tutored		(0) Student Absent

© Copyright by Greenwood, Delquadri, and Carta, 1997. All rights reserved.

READING RATE CHART

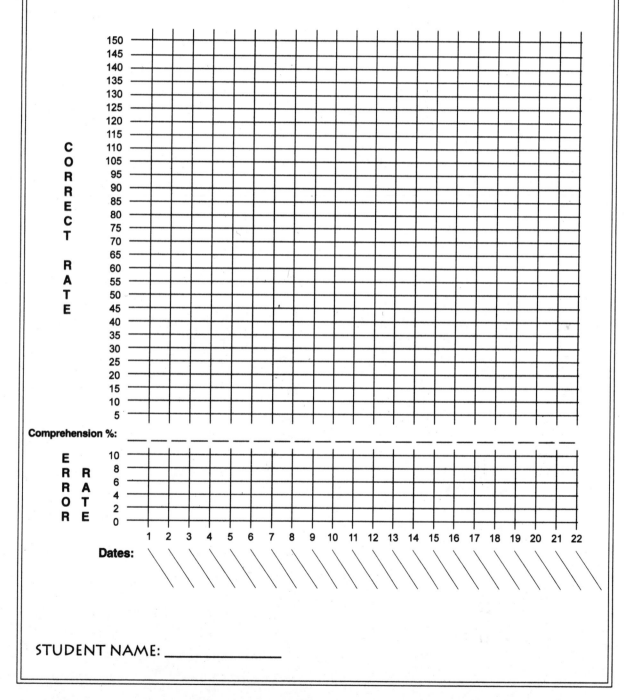

STUDENT NAME: _____

© Copyright by Greenwood, Delquadri, and Carta, 1997. All rights reserved.